# Buzzin Bards 2020

## A Manchester England Poetry Anthology

Edited by
James P. Wagner (Ishwa)

Buzzin Bards 2020

Published by Local Gems Press

www.localgemspoetrypress.com

**Buzzin Bards Yard President:**

Benjamin William Crisafulli (Ushiku)

**Bards International President:**

James P. Wagner (Ishwa)

*Dedicated to all poets in the Manchester, U.K. area!*

To Stevie
Happy Reading.
from
S. Jonah J. (:)
P

# Foreword

2020 has been an unusual year, even in Manchester where we pride ourselves on how we "do things differently here". The start of the year saw fantastic developments in poetry with The Meteor and Switchblade Society in particular giving us fantastic poetry events in what seems like a decade ago. We did however see how Manchester comes together in a crisis - with a groundswell of grassroots support for many fantastic venues such as The Peer Hat and The Frog and Bucket. We've also seen the theatres of Manchester come together as Greater Manchester Artist Hub.

If there's one thing we have more than rain and excellent artistry in this beautiful city of ours it would have to be compassion. Our ability to come together, support each other, and make our voices heard even against seemingly insurmountable odds is somewhat of a Mancunian specialty be it Peterloo, our blockade of slave picked cotton during the American Civil War, splitting the atom, making the first computer, or in more recent times how reds and blues alike were A City United in supporting free school meals for our most vulnerable in society. We face problems like a Piccadilly Gardens pigeon faces an unsuspecting forehead, but with a much better success rate.

Mancunians are natural poets and story tellers, so it is no surprise that our anthology has doubled in size since last year. While we won't be able to hold a physical launch at this time, we will commemorate our collective achievement with a digital launch - and we will also honour each and every one of you when we are able to do so in person.

~ Ushiku Crisafulli.

# Table of Contents

# Saqab Ahmad

## Lock Down World

Yellow Tape.
Different floor.
New guides.
lost time.
lock down.

New world.
Takes time.
Changing wave.
Goodbye tape.

Happy people.
Laughing loud.
Open hearts.
New reality .
Normal life.

---

Saqab is an emerging artist who likes to create art in many mediums. You can find him on Instagram.com/saqabart where he regularly updates new original art. He likes to write poems on varied subjects. These can be humorous, serious with the times we live in or about people of interest. He is a down to earth Manc full of smiles and life.

# Ged Austin

The calendar of now.
There is only one day on a calendar that truly exists and is real.
That is called today, the time of now that your five senses can see,
hear, smell, taste and feel.
The previous day before has passed and gone away, which in truth
means that it is dead.
The next day to become is called tomorrow and lives inside the
dreamers future head.
In the calendar of life you only have one day at a time.
So please make the best of it there and then before it fades away
forever into the sublime.

---

Ged austin known as the Manchester urban poem. Born in Manchester
in 1960. Loves writing all kinds of poetry. Left school with no
qualifications because I had dyslexia and no support was given at
school as to be fair I didn't know I had it and teachers weren't trained
to identify it. When I told a teacher I wanted to be a poet and writer he
laughed and said I had more chance being an astronaut so I didn't
write poetry until I was 29 years old.

# Eloïse Bennigsen

## The Mainline in January, 0658 am

Blackbirds click in the thick dank air,
faded blurs swirling through the fog
resting on the moist fences of terrace gardens.

Behind each garden the line lies like
a silent adder. The wires crack as the track
vibrates, and the first smeary train

slithers past. The birds rise screeching
into the sluggish sky. In the terraces
people shift in their beds as they wake.

---

Originally from Stockport, Eloïse Bennigsen is an English literature
and creative writing student at Lancaster University, and has been
writing poetry and prose since she was seven. Her work often focuses
on place and our interactions with surroundings; in particular, the
edges and boundaries of places.

# Sefton Booth

## Blue Spark

Today I found a bulb
And polished it from a smudge
And placed it in a projector
Illuminating the room
Taking us to dreamed up worlds

Today I found a bulb
And learnt how to screw it in
The flick of the switch
Lit up my darkest fears
And we tackled them head on

Today I found a bulb
I knew exactly what it was for
I stood and gripped the glass tight in my hand
And knew just what had to be done
As I gripped it tighter and tighter

Today I found a bulb
Today I made a difference
That difference was for you
That difference was in me
Today I found a bulb.

A local man who has just completed his 19th book. 16 of these were just realised in succession and are made up of a poetry experiment. The next story will be released and read to his children.

# Gino Brandolani

## The Scavenger Triumphs

Out on the Irwell's elbow
At Morns first open door
I saw a scrounging seabird
Best a nimrod Falcon
Fast high upon the soar.

In that clash of beak and claw
The Lord of stratos throne did fall
From empyrean kingdom tort tumble,
down far to Plebeian floor.

The paragon of Heavens felled,
by the feeder from the tip.
A victor shod in yellow web,
sans grant of talon to rend or tear or rip.

Hark this herald well I plea,
all you of wealth and say
Heed this caution lest your house be ransom,
Listen close, you of feet of clay

When home and young become a subject of
the patricians prize to prey.
Courage rose in the parent Gull

and the predator it did slay.
That freeman of the midden cawed
*"I have took  the day"*.

So oppidan bear up this charge
tell each ear along the way,
That when the tyrant hunter calls
we the poor will have our say.

---

A Self-deprecating Narcissist, fierce philosophical drinker and primarily absent thinker. This Seelveen wantonly purloins styles and structures and verbiage from the whole of the penned utterances of time to fill his pallet, fat. By this he eases his ability in allegory to equate the human experience to that which he witnesses in nature . His only saving grace is that he is aware of his own buffoon- ery and in that he gladly frolics.

# Dunstan Carter

## On the Edge of the Town

I'm balancing on the edge of the town,
A soft breeze hushing me nowhere,

Winding through the wasteland
And kicking loose stones,

Taken with solitude
And blown with hot dirt,

Across the ruined spot where
The soldiers wandered home.

I stop and stare at the ground,

The dry earth has risen and started to peak
Into small terracotta roofs pointing upwards,

Tumbleweed detritus skips across the mounds
And a wind whips its afternoon moan.

I sit on a fridge and get lost in the nothing,
I feel the groans from the monolithic industry all around,

I hear the heartbeats of hustling mice,
The scurry of beetles and a rumbling,

Bird song processed
All bent and reshaped;

An April rain falls and I'm inside the wet,
Loosened by breath,

Pulled into the dust from the factory floors,
The rhythmic grind of machines and the hiss of freed steam,

The perpetual thud of gnarled energy quaking,
The singing pistons and greased mechanisms,

Salt slowly dancing in the sweat of the bustle,
A hundred bass lines rotating,

Spinning generators harmonising with turbines
As transformers pump discords,

Furnaces howling as metal shards melt
And their fate drips like tears trapped in chaos.

There are workers here who've never left and rarely paused,
An electric sense of pride in nothing but grizzled routine,

I'm not sure what gets made here
But without it we're nothing.

Dunstan Carter is a poet and illustrator based in Stalybridge. His work has appeared in Penumbra magazine, Never Bury Poetry, irk and The Errorist, and in Macmillan Education's 'Inspired English 2 anthology'. He's currently working on a collection of poems called 'Idolised' inspired by some of the world's greatest music icons.

# Benjamin Cassidy

## Lessons

Mine's where the water's
free flowing
and tippling, streaming
towards where it's going

Mine's how sunlight cuts
shapes, moving
and dappling, mapping
all light's lawn it's mowing

Mine's inhaling scents
blooming, giving
their offerings, wafting
their ways in my being

Mine's the listening, watching and waiting,
the taking of time, merrily contemplating

Benjamin Francis Cassidy lives in Rusholme, Manchester, with his cat, Lucy. He writes reviews and articles for Sci-fi Pulse. He has had poetry published by Yaffle Press and Fly on the Wall Press, both Northwest England based. He has had criticism published by The High Window magazine and The Lake magazine. He's loved poetry since he was fist read nursery-rhymes as a child, and continues to.

# Lou Clarke

## Peel Here

Take time to peel here and scratch to reveal the prize
Life has been flying by
Distracted by entertainers
by political entrainers
A veneer of fear leaving some dumb,
some livid
And others asking 'why?'

Life  is what happens  while  others  plans  are busy making  you

And yet you rejoice in the singalong

Something wrong?

Oh come on,
Either choose to move or don't

But if the latter
try not to long too long for something...
else will always be waiting
To keep you in the infuriating

Reality presented

A present from the clock face to the cogs
To keep them turning
Churning out and burning out
An incessant feed of replacements
Procreating their way into the living labour hour

But you can be wise,
Take time to peel here (*eyes)
and scratch (*head)
to reveal the prize

# George Clayton

## Mary's House

Mary's house is empty now
She's gone to meet her maker
'For Sale' says the sign at the front window
But as yet there's been no taker

Her patch of lawn is overgrown
With dandelions and weeds
It's been a year since it was mown
Green fingers what it needs.

Nevermore will I glimpse her head
As she washes the pots after tea,
It makes you think about being dead,
Soon the same will happen to me.

But it's no good gazing over the fence
And thinking it's all very sad,
Against 'The Grim Reaper' there's no defence
If that upsets you - too bad!

After a lifetime as an artist, George began writing mostly nonsense poetry ten years ago. This poem is representative of his work.

# Ushiku Crisafulli

## Remembering how to smile

Are you ever so used to misery
that you become exhausted by happiness?
Muscles torn like forgotten heart strings
from joys long past known
then unknown.

They say it takes less muscles to smile than frown,
but have you ever pondered the shape, the tone?
Incandescent nightmares
become a lesion on my muscle memory.

Yet unhappiness is a parasite, that one day inhabited me,
so I shall become buff with gratitude,
and remember how to smile again.

---

Ushiku Crisafulli is a chef, poet, playwright, actor, performance artist, musician and founder of the OpenMind Collective. He runs the various Bards projects throughout the UK, and is also currently working on a hip-hop theatre exploration of the year of his Asperger's diagnosis called Unmasked.

# Sarra Culleno

## Une Villanelle Pour Ma Belle

Since before youth so long ago,
when red we used to paint the town,
Duchesse, you so well I know.

A ma ami, a debt I owe,
for mandy-halves which made us clown.
Benevolence we felt to show.

Tables turned and strung our bow,
dancing girls who'd not come down
from Brave New Worlds we grew to know.

Canal Street, the North's Soho,
we earned the pearly Queen Town Crown;
we had right royal shapes to throw.

Ma copine, my rainbow.
And still you wipe away my frown
since another life so long ago.

May the BPMs never slow.

# Steven Duffy

## Unconditional Love

As she looks into his eyes,
Sees herself reflected.
Awestruck by her own beauty.
Her radiance.
At long last someone had noticed.
After so many years.
Alone.
Remembers.
The warmth and adoration.
The love and praise,
Freely given by so many,
For so long.
A bundle of joy.
A glorious innocence.
A beaming magnificence.
Shining.
Long before she understood,
The words.
Praised and worshipped,
For just existing.
Living.
A gift.
A promise of greatness.

Unfulfilled potential.
In everyone who witnessed,
A sense that all is right in the world.
Until one day.
The compliments and soft touches,
Became  accusations and roughness,
Disrespectful and obnoxious,
Poisonous and toxic.
And so.
She built walls.
Covered them with spikes
And shards of glass,
Rained fire on those foolish
Enough to come close.
Became closed.
A secret.
Buried deep within the fortress of her flesh.
The defences became a challenge,
For those coming of age.
Wishing to prove their manhood.
The unworthy set themselves
to task.
To breach the citadel and steal the treasure buried deep within.
Many found themselves cast
on the rocks below.
She laughed.
A hollow sound.
A warning to those foolish enough
to risk all for a promise.
Until one day.

He came.
A prince.
With eyes of burnt umber
And a jaw carved from granite.
His weapons?
Sweet words.
Truths not heard for many years,
Began to chip away at her fortifications.
Such pleasant attacks.
Began to crack and break though.
Until.
She found herself exposed.
Vulnerable.
The child that once was.
Only looking for what the world had promised long ago.
Defeated by hollow promises and
The intoxicating dream of
unconditional love

# Bryan Dunne

## Northerner Spirit

In times of crisis a Northerner I'd rather be, I'm not saying the
South ain't right it just isn't right for me.
We rally round our loved ones, the old, the sick and poor.
We'll do the shopping for them and drop it at their door.
They'll offer to give us the money, we'll say stick it in your purse
or wallet this one's free,
When I'm on the bones of my arse they'll do the same for me.

Up North were often seen as the poor cousins of the South,
Living day to day, living hand to mouth.
But what they don't understand is we're rich beyond belief, we
come from a land of pie, chips and gravy, jam butties and corned
beef.

Music the arts and industry is where we really shine,
The Beatles, Oasis, Arctic Monkeys, Stone Roses and the
Beautiful South.. who just need a little time.
Lowry and Pankhurst, Turing cracked a code or two.
Victoria Wood, Beatrix Potter and some Band Take That who did
a song with Lulu.

Johnny Vegas, Manford, Peter Kay and Bishop with a joke to tell.
There's something in the water up north we've got a magic Well.

Humour by the bucket load, regardless if we have a pot to piss in.
Just the fact your from the North already means your winnin.

From a pan of scouse to Yorkshire Tea, an Eccles Cake or a Stotty
or three.
Kendal mint cake and Wenslydale Cheese and of course a
Yorkshire pudding will never fail to please.

Northern delights are a beautiful sight,
Not the Aurora Borialis but kicking out time down your local on a
Friday night.

So embrace that Northern spirit and really let it out,
It's grim up North is what they say,
But they don't know nowt.

---

Bryan Dunne is a creative person with a passion for poetry, acting and art. Bryan works for children's services helping young people with the situations they find themselves in.

Elizabeth Gibson

## Farawayland

The frogs here are truly relentless,
screech, screech, love and dive,
splashing the burnt pond rocks
where dense orange cats suffer.
The spider-shaped student dorm
on a mountain ledge, nobody else
anywhere near – you could *yell* –
the polleny air would swallow
every note, let you take it all out.
No ruckus of birds, the deer on signs
never showing in the still night,
crickets an alarm you stop hearing.
Storms are vicious when they come,
wildfires show beauty no mercy.
The bomb, however, is faraway.
When it happens, it is late here.
I cannot process it until the names
start coming, and in slithers guilt,
loss of belonging, not being there
when the pain came to my own land.

Elizabeth Gibson is a poet and performer based in central Manchester. She has won a Northern Writers' Award and has been published in journals including Cake, The Cardiff Review, Confingo, Popshot and Strix, as well as the *Mancunian Ways* anthology from Fly on the Wall Press. She tweets at @Grizonne.

# Ben Gilman

## Do the Write Thing

First thing, remember to breathe,
Start writing before your ideas leave,
Stay calm, keep your lines organic,
Oh my God! What rhymes with panic!
You're building momentum, when you're stopped in shock,
Our good friend arrives, old writer's block,
He steals your words, grabs hold of your tongue,
This five-line poem is taking too long,
Take a break, if you must, to find the words you seek,
An hour should be enough, and there goes the week,
Now is the time to focus and think,
Finish the poem, hope it doesn't stink,
Turn off my phone, no feeling bitter,
But first I'll check Facebook, Instagram and Twitter,
Now I'm writing free, my words are flowing,
With every second, my confidence growing,
Now, as I approach the end of my writing,
I'd better leave a message, oooh how exciting,
For this lesson works in every city, village or town,
If you have an idea, fucking write it down!

Ben Gilman is a twenty-nine-year-old English Literature and History student from Leigh. Ben has written poetry about a range of topics, from political rants to more personal topics, such as overcoming anxiety. A big fan of open mic nights, Ben has performed across Greater Manchester in events organised by Write Out Loud and Bad Language.

# John A Gilman

## Unspoken

Tell a big lie,
Shout it.
Scream it,
Louder and louder.
Overlap the echoes,
Repeated reverberation.
Write it,
Send it,
Imprint it,
Seal it inside.
Remember it,
Recall it.
Love it,
Cherish it.

Tell a big lie,
Shout it,
Scream it,
Until it becomes,
A small truth.

JA Gilman is originally from the sunny climes of Yorkshire, loves music, board gaming and magic the gathering. Plays the drums in an eighties covers band (TheHats)

# Allan Graham

## Don't Give Up

When the odds are stacked against you
When you've taken all you can
When you're heart is tired and broken
When you've reached your journey's end
When you're battered and bruised and on your knees
When your face is in the dust
When all your friends desert you
When there's no-one left to trust
When losing is better than winning
When Death is a welcome friend
When you think you've reached your limit
Stop!…And think again
There's a seed of life inside you
There's a power deep within
Breathe it; Feel it
Love and laugh
Learn to live again
Get off your knees
And rise like God
Give Death a mocking glare
Laugh at your adversities
Rejoice at lessons learned
Face your foes

Defeat your fears
And you will win this day
And you will win a thousand more
With your strength to guide the way

---

Allan Graham is a poet/writer living in Saddleworth. Born in Leigh, Lancashire, surrounded by coal mines he was the first child not to follow his descendants into this tough life. Surrounded by books from a very early age, Allan, won a scholarship to Leigh Grammar School and then worked in IT for the next 40 years, which he still does at Saddleworth School. He has written many poems on different subjects, plus four children's novels. One of which he wrote with students from Saddleworth School. He is a regular visitor to the classes within the school and to surrounding Primary Schools, reading his poetry and extracts from his novels, trying to inspire and enthuse the next generation of writers. He has organised three literary festivals and one of his poems, 'ONCE UPON A TIME' is published on a website 'No Glory' (www.noglory.org) alongside literary greats - Rudyard Kipling, Wilfred Owen, Siegfried Sassoon and Carol Anne Duffy.

# D. Greenwood

## Dead Crow

A crow trap hides in the long grass
Blades caress the slender wooden struts
Or clamber through chickenwire
Tantric knots lulling an obsidian
Ship to smash her hull on jagged
Rocks and sit marooned in green swell

For months the trap lay bare
Disappointment palpable

Then, one day, trudging through snow
To where the chicken coop stood I saw,
Bound in the wire, a lump of coal
Cut straight from the cold rock-face
The sleek form of the crow

Back to the house, carving trenches
Through knee-high snow I sprinted and stumbled
For Grandad.

He couldn't match my pace and was a long time reaching us.
I had time to stare into the bubble
Of crude oil dripping from the night-sky
She, in turn saw me.

Grandad, now beside me, his
Large hand on my shoulder
In the other dozed his rifle
No less ugly with its back broken
Terror flew, flapping and screaming in my cage
Though the bird just looked with quiet curiosity.

I begged grandad to leave her alone
But, with sad eyes he told me not to look

I turn away, hear the hollow click
Of the rifle's teeth then the deadly
Dry cluck of its gunpowder tongue.
With salt in my eyes I turn
To see grandad throw the bristling black corpse
Over a privet hedge
And I see the crow
For a split second
Crucified against the cold, hard
February sky

---

D. Greenwood was born under the shadow of Pendle Hill, Lancs but currently resides in the exciting metropolis of Manchester. He has been writing poetry for longer than he thought but has only recently realised and is performing, when able, as far as the eye can see (Within the North West of England).

# Said Hany

## Remember You

Every morning,
When the breeze caresses the dew,
Like your touch, I remember you,
When the sun disperses the hue,
Like your warmth, I remember you.
Every evening,
When silence enriches the few,
Like your thoughts, I remember you,
When shelter embraces the two,
Like your eyes, I remember you.

---

Said is a retired paediatrician who writes poetry based on his strong belief in artistic expression. He has published few books in philosophy, theology, mathematics and history. All his poems are uniformly rhymed, and most of them are in couplets.

# Mark Heathcote

**Rainy days**

What streets have seen more tears?
More grief than the cobbled streets of Manchester
my heart was once a flower meadow,
but now the prettiest littlest thing that grows
in-between the cracks are purple-blue Milkwort's
otherwise known as snakeroots; this is how
our paths cross and combine until-the-way is lost.

Jostling for space for sunlight
overshadowing others more shrivelled-out trampled-upon.
We appear from our cracks like fat wriggling earthworms,
sensing a virginal world is unfolding,
but then along comes a blackbird
or a red robin and all our sunshine,
rainy days and tears are gone.

Mark Andrew Heathcote is adult learning difficulties support worker, his poetry has been published in many journals, magazines and anthologies, he resides in the UK, from Manchester, he is the author of "In Perpetuity" and "Back on Earth" two books of poems published by a CTU publishing group ~ Creative Talents Unleashed

Edward Heathman

**From the Bottom of the Ocean**

The first time
I took you
was the morning after.

We were awfully hungover
and didn't care
about anything,

except the warm discovery
of a new man
in your bed.

Your cat showed me
an envying stare
from the duvet
before you rolled her off.

Yes, my body
was trying
to accommodate
your body.

Every inch

of you
had an Atlantic pressure.

Canadian geese
honked
in the canal
beyond your window.

You squeezed me so tightly
I was never so glad
to have bones.

Ignoring the ache
in my gracilis.
O to bear

you like this
was such an annihilating
blessing.

I knew then, you were the sort
water runs off of,

and me,
I was the one
the water
goes
right through.

Edward Heathman was born in 1995. He grew up in South Wales and is currently studying for an MA in Creative Writing at the University of Manchester. He has a YouTube channel where he talks about books: youtube.com/Gagging4Lit

# Callum Hogan

**Awareness**

You are the mountain so tall,
You are the bear which hibernates,
You are the tiniest of insect,
You are the flower which radiates.

You are all the seasons,
You are the Ocean deep,
You are the buzzing bee,
You are the frog that leaps,

You are the Sun in The Heavens,
You are the birds that fly,
You are the flowing river,
You are the energy that Never Dies,

You are the ripples in the waves,
You are the stars in the distance,
You are the leaf that falls in Autumn,
You are all in existence.

Callum Hogan, 22. An amateur poet with a passion for deep and insightful poetry. He thinks poetry is a powerful tool of self-awareness, self- reassurance and communication. He values both the abstract and the concrete and finds the beauty in everything.

# Philippa Hogg

## Temporizing

It's so much harder to waste a day in winter,
harder still when that's all there is to do.
Days stream through curtains, half drawn,
a glimpse of invariable grey
drifting.
Rain rolls over the tidal lull
of tangled clouds,
wringing out a storm.
Droplets that swoop down and splatter
on windows, shut tight in wait,
spill over into dark pools
brimming
with the remnants of a day
Spent.

---

Philippa Hogg is an EFL teacher recently returned to Manchester after teaching English in Japan. She loves nature and wildlife photography and is heavily influenced by the landscape of the English countryside. She has been writing poems since she was in high school and studied creative writing in university.

# Jack Horner

## Dream state

*A montage of thoughts jotted down from vivid dreams I had once I had started taking citalopram. Some lines are an acknowledgment to my journey through mental health recovery too.*

I cramped, I stamped, I daily walked a plank
But then I pulled a tattered torn rip cord
I was a master of boredom a vacant void collector
And time lied to me until three to tease slumber


I gazed at walls in a trance of carrion calls
secrets arrived from stories a stored
I answered them abundantly in their hoards
Why can't I be a shopping channel surfer

I watched feather bombs explode over heather
Barricade walls were made of lotus flowers
I sat on a see saw in a deep-sea diver's suite
While an owl kissed a stopped clocks face

I built totem poles made of terrapin heads
Men with mushroom heads slept in mushroom beds
A masquerade ball magician wore boxing gloves

I removed revelations from a rusty green bucket

Tomorrow I will drink tea from a garden sprinkler
I will sculpt alien life form from grubby blue tac
I will stare at spacemen kissing intergalactic mermaids
And I will burst a peapod bubble in a cactus garden

I then covered my face in clay dirt to hide the hurt
I continuously called a self-created number from a telephone
kiosk
A charmer space farmer sold popper pills and potions
And I ran backwards up a steep cobbled hill

A pink flamingo then professed landslide
The pharmacist let psychedelic colours collide
A smiling crocodile played a piano
And a psychic lemon escaped to tomorrow

I departed this ambivalent false fairy tail
Scenes interrupted by ice cream van cries
I emptied mosaic mind bins with extended limbs
And consider the Russian doll syndrome I created

A piece by Jack AKA Leon the pig farmer, a Manchester based Beat poet who began creative writing and performing spoken word a little over 15 months ago as a consequence of suffering from mental health issues and beginning a journey to recovery. A performer who is as comfortable in the spopken word environment as he is expressing his creativity on the music circuit as a spoken worsmith.

# Elizabeth Horrocks

**Sea Poem** *(Hiraeth)*

The sea calls to me.
Far from the red cliffs of my inland home
the gulls' way, the whales' way
sings its seductive song.

The white topped waves hiss and surge,
tuned to the pulse of my blood.
With my inward ear I hear, always,
the mewling cry of wheeling gulls.

The rustle of wind in these inland trees
is the sussuration of sea on sand:
the damping of the air becomes
sea-spray reaching me from a far-off coast.

I build barriers and cultivate content
to keep its sounds from me
in this place that has everything I want.

Except the sea. Except the sea

Born in South Wales, Elizabeth Horrocks has lived most of her adult life in Cheshire. She taught English locally at Hyde Clarendon College, as well as other places. She has published three novels - a trilogy for young adults based on the Arthurian Legends brought up to date, and her poetry has been published in many places including Writing Magazine and Acumen. She was BBC Mastermind champion in 1974, and has appeared in several of the anniversary programmes.

Faye Kavanagh

## The Storm

She rides the waves, a storm of broken love again
Her world comes crashing down
Her heart broken into pieces like a shipwreck tossed to the bottom
of the sea
She will rescue herself
Floating on the driftwood she calls life
There's a break in the clouds
Calm waters at last
The sun and the warm breeze gently dance on her face
She's survived the storm
A warrior to her own pain
Maybe, just maybe
She will love again

---

Faye is a working, single mother of six children, she lives in Stretford, Manchester. She is three years into her recovery which is when she started writing poetry and loves writing poetry, listening to music and gardening.

# Ian Leslie

## You'll Never Walk Alone

A phone in post-mortem on David Moyes
Made grown men revert to smudge faced boys.
 Utd fans given a chance to reminisce,
The greatest times they undoubtedly miss.

About their memories and the feelings they evoke;
Celebrities (and Terry Christian) warmly spoke.
 Solksjaer at Barca; Cantona's Wembley
But, some offered a more transcendent memory

 Ronaldo, not Cristiano in this tale
But the now sturdy South American then playing for Real
And, they chanted *his* name as one of their own
When he left the pitch, he didn't walk alone.

Consider those moments bigger than sport
When it's more than football you report
One recalled Michael Knighton buying the club
He appeared on the field doing kick-ups
New belief before the cheers stopped to ring
Prematurely deflowered by yet another false spring
But, they chanted his name as one of their own
On the pitch, that day, he didn't walk alone.

My greatest memory is not my first game
Backed by the Salford guttural refrain
Nor collected moments of sublime brilliance
From a still svelte, mobile Brazilian

Not a debut win that promised so much
Nor a dodgy businessman with a great first touch
But when the Hillsborough campaign came in 89…
And the Stretford End began to chime.

 We chanted their song as one of our own
When they paced the pitch, they didn't walk alone.
And they'll never walk alone
And 'You'll Never Walk Alone'.

# Jonny Lindsey

## Proud To Be From The North

The North is just a collection of sheds built around Tesco's.
We keep it classy up here
Chips n gravy, 'av it alfresco
The North has been neglected
For over a decade
It's reflected
Not by nature - that never caused recessions
but in man made bad decisions
Like agreeing to have supermarket chains
Swallow up our land
So someone in a suit can get a backhand,
Their only purpose
Is to bleed a towns shops dry
The town cries
But it's too late, it's empty buildings &
Cash converters
It used to be rolling hills, bustling streets that sold flowers,
clothes & 'taters
They've got the country by the bollocks now
Nice one Britain, si'thi'laters
By the time people care,
Like Boris Johnson's hair - it dies.
And by the time people who've had their cake and eaten it
have died & gone t'Heaven

I'd still sooner be Northern than say Scones wrong
And be born in Devon.

Born in Accrington, Jonny Lindsey looks to promote the North of England via poems & drinking pints. He does not like Toffs but does enjoy coffee. Find more of his poems on his Instagram: Jonnylindseythefirst

Dorinda MacDowell

## A Place I Never Knew

Misty, black and white photograph.
Looking at it I'm transported
into the seeming serenity
of this bucolic scene
and it makes me sigh
because
we don't see lanes like that any more

For a moment, I am that woman in the photograph
standing in the doorway of her small cottage
holding a baby in her arms

What appears idyllic most likely
was nothing of the sort
because
life was hard, then, when you were poor

So I don't stay in my temporary day-dream any longer

I blink and the photograph dims
and seems to disappear
into some half-remembered sanctuary

of an age gone by
promising serenity, denying harsh reality

I leave a place I never knew

---

I am wife, Mother, Grandma, lover of life and words.

# Alicia Maggs

## Grandad

It's been 2 months since you grew your wings and flew away
I still think about you every single day
I hope you see me way up there
Just can't seem to find my air
I really hope I'm making you proud
Even though my thoughts get really loud
Sometimes I just cry
Ask thin air why
Why couldn't you just stay?
I'm not even religious and I try to pray
Told us that it was too late
Something had already decided your fate
I tried to do everything I could
But in the end it was no good
My whole body is filled with regrets
Waking up at night in cold sweats
Wishing I would've said this and that
Replaying that last chat

You loved to watch all the seguls fly around
They were your favourite bird, hands down
You'd take us to the beach every time we came
It's heartbreaking knowing our trips will never be the same

It's gonna be hard that your not the first face we'll see
Sitting on the bench with such glee
Waiting for the bus to get there
Why is this life so unfair?
You were the best grandad I could've ever had
For the memories you've gifted me I'll be forever glad
Even when the kiosk near you shut down
You still found over a 100 sodavands just so you didn't have to see me frown
To have you here with us for just one more day
I still don't think I'd know what to say
I know that I'll see you again
I just don't really know when
So for now I'll talk into empty space
Saying everything I wish I could've face to face...

# Edith Marion

## Public House

We live inside bricks.
Crippled by fear.
Constantly sick.
But, can't leave here.
Fumes are toxic.
Thoughts, not clear.
Life is not magic.
But we can fake cheer.
Tell 'em again, just stop it.
Yet, no-one hears.
Next level logic.
Escape from my peers.
Why can't I escape it?
Blinded by tears.
A switch gets flicked.
Suddenly...
I drink beer.
Alcoholic...
Attack, verbal spears.

Edith Marion is a poetic writer from Manchester. Her stories are influenced by the sounds of the city & all of her crazy inhabitants, as well as American hip hop culture. She has been writing poems & short-stories for over 20 years.

John E Marks

## A Blessing

Brother Sun and Sister Moon
Shine on the people of this world.
Let them recall the smells of spring
On cold and drear November days.

And let them hear the baby's cry,
That all the hounds of hell defy,
And give them all the boons of love –
For love is really all we are –

The tiny gestures — the glance, the word –
That will in memory recur.
And deep amidst the fears of night
Bring a holy glimmer of delight.

Leila Martin

**Pieces of you**

You won't pack the TV yet. Your face skewers into it, ghoulish
from its glow.
You mutter you can still hear her in the creaks and ticks of this
freshly skinned home;
this home
that turned your memories against you.
I creak upstairs to your room and her wardrobe, retrieve pieces
of her,
faded glamour in sleek handfuls, shrieking softly on the rail.

I tell you it will be ok, but you hunker into the sofa and stab the
remote and
gaze at false families playing out false dramas. I pour cold tea
down the sink, then
smother her fluted china in brown paper.

You watch the TV with the lights off.
The hall rattles a strange echo that
catches at my stride.
A fresh start, I say. I try on a smile; sit on the sofa beside you.
You nod and your eyes slide back
to the brightly-scripted banter and clinking crockery.

Your new bungalow has your old sofa and a 32 inch plasma with

surround-sound.
You settle there, at once a fixture.
A fresh start, I say. You glance and nod, your eyes earnest, but
behind them I sense
a door closing.

In the car I kill the radio's chatter. The street's façade
is always the same and suddenly
waspish-strange.
My keys jingle a greeting
that goes unanswered.
There's one box left on the counter.
I pull the marker from my pocket and
label it *Fragile.*

---

Leila is a copywriter from Salford. An avid reader and writer of poetry, Leila also writes short stories and has ghost-written articles on a range of topics from aesthetics to self-help. On the rare occasions she's not in front of her laptop, Leila enjoys hiking to ancient sites and wild places.

# Alan McKean

## Panic Buying

I went out to the shops earlier, just to see what I could buy
The shelves were just a desert, I began to wonder why.

The breadman must've been ill, he really, really must
No muffins, toasters, there were nowt except some bags of crusts.

I got round to the tea aisle and, just to assuage my greed
I bought two extra boxes that we didn't really need.

Condiments were easy, salt, olive oil and mustard
But when I went to look for some, I couldn't find the custard

The bakery was shameful, that really opened my eyes,
'Cos judging by the gaps, there'd been a run on apple pies.

I could have bought a hammer drill, a welding mask, or griddle
Or other real essential stuff there, in the Middle of Lidl.

They'd sold out of sanitizer, and antiseptic soap
They'd even empty spaces where they'd had soap-on-a-rope.

Now, toilet rolls' an issue, for nowt will come of it,
You don't need fifty packs of four if you're just satisfying
your needs.

Shelves were empty, trolleys full, all tills taking the strain
Of two years' worth of Morrisons stuff – looked like a
wagon train.

The small trolleys lie lonely in their windswept trolley bay
For ev'ryone's using big uns, to wisk they buys away.

And not just single trolleys, these shoppers hunt in packs
They're even running out of logs that're sold in hessian sacks.

So, we worry about Corona, it's certainly made me think
Back to the days of my childhood when it was just a fizzy drink.

The media's ecstatic, as they daily grind out fear
I wonder what we'll remember at this same time next year.

When colds and flu arrive, as they do each winter time
Will it give me a chance to write another cracking rhyme?

Us oldies are advised to keep ourselves indoors,
Or will they simply round us up and dump us on the moors?

So, next time I go shopping, to make sure that I feel fine
I'll simply fill my trolley up with whisky, beer and wine.

And although it may not help me, as I slump, drunk, in my chair
I'll simply raise another glass 'cos I won't really care

So I'll let the media panic in papers, on Tv

And raise two Lancashire fingers, shouting "stop annoying me!"

Right,
just nipping to the Co-op for.....
Well,
Anything really

---

Alan is retired, and lives at the outer edges of Greater Manchester, in Littleborough. He has been writing for around eighteen years, and his poetry comes from what he sees around him in the hills, with occasional foray into the city. He likes to write in any format really, it depends what falls off his pencil, but he does enjoy writing the occasional Lancashire dialect poem.

# George Melling

9.15 on a Tuesday night in May,
large gin and tonic with ice,
packet of ready salted crisps
and a wooden bench,
splinter-less,
to rest my weary bones.

I sit with
 the peace of a slowly darkening sky
and barely a wisp of cloud
between me and
a thin crescent of a moon
that seems reluctant
 to
show itself,
maybe it's self-isolating.

 My glass,
time for a refill
as the gentle buzz of inebriation
starts to take over
at ten o'clock
and a pinky glow
perhaps promises a nice day tomorrow
or

it could be me getting
slightly tipsy,
it being quite a nice batch of
London Dry Gin.

I can hear the slight buzz of
distant traffic,
more than we've had for quite a few weeks
as the shackles of lockdown
are eased,
I hope not prematurely,
and a blackbird sings its song of bedtime
to its mate
as a garland of
solar fairy lights,
pinned to the conifers by
Ar Sharon,
do what they're supposed to do
and come on,
acting as a backdrop
to my fountain pen and pad
writing these words by themselves
as I disappear
into the fug
of pissed.

Goodnight.

George Melling, also known as Th'Owd Chap, lamenting the loss of his free TV licence after turning 75 a couple of years ago, lives with Buttons the cat and his memories. His fountain pen is always to hand to catch those whispers of words that have a habit of appearing in the most mundane of places.

# Anisha Minocha

## An Ode of Adolescence

When my eyelids droop-
like flower petals under the pressured weight of a teardrop.
and love plays more-
like a game of hide and seek, within the board of
snakes and vanishing ladders

bare hands- rugged and sweet- slip
to absorb this tear stained cheek
torn emotions- scramble
to caress brief notions, of phantom like dreams.

I wander
beneath the cover of my
rampaging, rampaging
constantly changing
country.
I wonder
if this is some ill health
or clumsy teenage stealth.

Anisha is a 17 year old passionate about writing poetry and exploring the power of words. She has performed spoken word poetry at the Royal Exchange Theatre in 'Letters to the Earth' and written articles on religion, social media and events in a local newspaper. As well as being winning poetry competitions such as #periodsinpandemics, she has work published in a magazine for Northern young voices, she blogs for students and writes her own creative pieces for her blog: https://ajmwritesonline.wordpress.com/ Twitter: @Anisha_Jaya

# David Morgan

## The Art of Deception

To look into the eye but not the soul
To grasp the hand firmly but not warmly
To speak with certainty but without feeling
To hear without listening
To remember the name but not the face
To act the part but not yourself
To agree wholeheartedly but not commit
To say you will but with no intent
To flatter idiots but bite your tongue
To smile but hide your assassin's knife
To walk tall but crawl when not observed
To dish it out but cry yourself to sleep.

---

Dave Morgan is a Bolton-based writer, organiser and fundraiser. He co-founded Write out Loud (2002) and Live from Worktown (2014) with whom he has promoted many festivals of music and the spoken word. His short collection Chuang Tse's Caterpillar (Flapjack Press 2016) contains a selection of new, previously published and prize winning poems.

# Alexander N Morrison

## PoeTRY !

What is it that blocks a persons mind !
It always wants to be released to somewhere else
Like the caged bird set it free......
Impediments are only walls you have to climb over
Doors you have to unlock and open
Visions you want to see...
Feelings you want to express.....
That moment.....that picture...that ambiance
Forget that Iambic Mechanicalness....
Be.....Be.......Being.....DO IT....
Go on be a ....POE...TRY !

Jam
Totally enraptured
Ambiance unbound
Deeelightful
An amalgam of pleasure
Nectar of the Gods
That taste buds devour
Sense.ational
A delight of succulence
A texture of Love
A rememberance of things past
A total ambrosiastic experience

Pure....Pure.......Puree Decaadence


Ode to Covid 19 !
Strange days
  A period of voidness
A journey into the unknown
    Stay Home-k e e p   A p a r t
Be ALERT
  The noise of silence
No hmmm or brrrrr of 'Normality'
  The absence of habitual routiness
But nature's dulcet tones resound
  Awakening to the excitement of nothing
Freedom but not Freedom....Trapped
  Groundhog Day
A sporadic masked population
  Walking in a Zombie like Dystopian world
Broken by the sound of clapping
  Government 'Lockdown' ...'Letdown'.....
Must go ..I've got a Delivery Slot' ...!

# Kay Murfett

I want to be caught in the clap of the universe.
And sprinkled back into space.
Into dust.
Into nothing.
Like a moth that chased the sun.
And wept for it could not reach.

---

Kay is a Wednesday's child who is full of woe. 27 year old fierce romanticist. That is, of course, when she's not in the office.

Jonah Newton

**Mirror Man**

A man for the North of England
they wanted –
a statue to stand on the hills
to look across the open moors
a symbol of goodwill

A modern-day work-of-art
they wanted –
a symbol of hope for us all
and so I stand here watching
an icon, some thirty feet tall

A man for all seasons
they wanted –
so look well, and maybe you'll see
reflections of all kinds of sadness
a world that is all but free

A man made of mirrors
they wanted –
so crystal and clear in this place
so gaze at my glass angle features –
perhaps you will see your own face

Jonah Newton is a Creative and Technical Writer from Cheshire, England. Has had stories, articles, and poems published in several magazines in the UK and USA, including 'Outlaw', 'The Spoof', '330 Words', 'Writer's Muse', 'Longshot Island', 'UNFIT', 'UNREAL', and 'The Journal of Irreproducible Results'. He is continually enthused by the wealth of wonderful stories which are told by people every day.

# Lisa O'Hare

## The City Shines - An Ode to Manchester

The city shines
As drizzle swaggers down
We just pull up our hoods
Our Manchester crowns

Cobble filled potholes
Dodged better than our best strikers
Nothing can stop us
On our way to our nights out

The weather is wet
But the wit is dry
Our hearts always full
Heads always high

But this place in the sun
Fizzes like vimto
That's when our city
Really puts on its best show

Glass towers glisten
Bars overflow
Sounds fill our streets

Everyone glows

As we know sun is fleeting
Our sun is so glorious
We soak it all in
Knowing the rain is more notorious

We put on our shades
Forget our brollies exist
Live in that moment
As sunshine should never be missed

Lisa O'Hare started sharing her writing in 2019 and she has since been regularly performing her work at events such as Verbose, Testify and Speak Easy. Two of her poems have been featured on BBC Radio Manchester's Upload show. She can be found on Instagram @leohare and on Twitter @Lisaohare_0.

# Allan Openshaw

## Homing Pigeon

It's been several years since
I muddled through
The drag of grey skies, and, losing my way,
I sense a kind of flight
In your nervous movements. Are you impressed this easily
By the glance of a near-stranger –
A near-stranger whose eyes seem homely
And lived-in?

Across the polished table
And several drinks
Our eyes recognised a common ground

Where
We both had met

Where
I would return someday…

Now
Ten years later,
Where tenderness heals all wounds
And love replaces the weals

With domesticity
I'm the one
To get into a flap
And let the cocked eye
of homeliness slip.

Losing my way?
A glance over several drinks?
No intentions of disloyalty?

How easy it is now
To be brought back
Down to earth: the common ground
Where I can always return.

I've never lost the instinct.

Allan is from Leigh. His interest in writing was sparked by the poems of Arthur Rimbaud, the song lyrics of David Bowie, and the novels of Hermann Hesse. Allan's work has been published in 'Brake' (*Community Arts North West*); and 'The Individual Spoke' (*Riot Stories*), a Paul Weller-funded poetry anthology.

Roy Page

## Docks and Quays

When I was a kid, growing up
In old Salford Town
Our street was always empty
With no cars to be found
They were play streets for the children
Playing "kick Can" and "Rally Vo"
And twenty-a-side Footy games
How times are different now

From the end of our street, you could see the Docks
And the Manchester Ship Canal
With Ships bringing goods from around the world
To Buy and Trade and Sell
Thousands of men moved Millions of Tons
Of Iron, Stone and Earth
Building Bridges and locks and digging the Docks
They all came for the work.

When Queen Victoria "cut the tape" in 1894
She opened up a gateway
And the World stepped through the door
For sixty years the Docks were booming
But slowly, over time
Ships got bigger, Containers took over

There was a gradual decline

My Uncle Jack worked on the Docks
Driving a Robell and laying down plates
For almost twenty years
He walked through those Dock gates

When the Docks were busy and work was a plenty
There was a sense of pride
When the Dock gates closed for the very last time
Part of Salford died

Now today, fifty years on it's quite a different scene
The Dockers are gone but in their place
Has risen Salford Quays
They saved the Docks and fixed the locks
And made the water clean
Yes Salford can be proud again
Of what it has achieved

It's a place where people live and work
Once again "The place to be"
With Museums, Theatre, a Media City
And a home for the BBC
A Water Sports Centre with Swans swimming by
Buildings of Glass reaching up to the sky
And across the water (hear the roar off the crowd)
Lies the "Theatre of Dreams"
Sir Matt would be proud
And if my Uncle Jack was here today

I know he would be pleased
To see the progress that's been made
Down on Salford Quays.

Roy Page.   64 years old.  Born in Salford, lived overlooking the
Docks.  Have been writing poetry for around 5 years.

# Khyati Patel

## A Poetical Love Affair

I keep searching for you my love
My thirst, lust, knowledge to know you
Is so great, so powerful right now, I'm like
a junky craving a fix intravenous
You were like Mars, I was like Venus

You saved me you see, when the nights were long
I was so far from home, lonely, dazed and confused
You came just then, a warm embrace, thus did chase
Those demons in the dark away, your verse
Seductive, emotions explicitly displayed

Sometimes I travel back in time
Looking for new rhymes, past times
To numb this pain, that rush I crave
Makes me feel whole again, everyday I pray
You will find your way here and save me

I discovered you at seventeen, our love
Affair then started, never completely departed
Just lost at points, heart hollow and aching
Needed to draw you close again
Feel a beautiful flow
Peace, calm, healing for you to bestow.

---

Khyati's love affair with poetry started at 17 in New Zealand when she had to write pieces for A level English. She had never written poetry before then. Her English teacher was impressed with her work and it created for her, both a form of therapy, and ceaseless joy.

# David Prestbury

## Down memory lane

"Can you see 'thingymijig' over there -
You know 'oojimacallit' ?"

"Oh! 'whatsisname' you mean?"
"Yes oojit? With his 'thingymibob' on -

"He looks a right 'so and so'-
"Hold on - here comes old 'dooins'

"On his 'what not? -
"I think his memory's gone you know?"

"Yes I think so too –
'Lets go to 'erm you know who's?"

"Down how do you say it –
" Oh! It's on the 'tip of mi tongue -

Beginning with 'M' something? -
Bloody Hell! Lane! ?" ......

Dave Prestbury was born in East Manchester, where he lived his childhood days. He has had four poetry books published; *The Donkey Stone and Dolly Blue Days, Oasis and the Twisted Wheel, Hidden by the Clouds* and *For Our Children.* His poetry is drawn from true life experience when growing up in 50's/60's Manchester. Living now on The Rock in Bury, he is currently working on a collaborative poetry book featuring selected poems written by himself, daughter, grand-daughter and late mother (four generations)."

Megan Rawson

## Looks like Rain

she has a nasty habit
of looking like the weather:
grey clouds
in her ashen cheeks;
as she stumbles downstairs,
mumbled apologies
broken under the sound of a coming rain.
but as the day brightens,
so does she.
her sunshine smile a pleasure for all to see.
those rosy cheeks were famous
in the beaming summer sun.
but afternoon rains slowly wash the glow away,
and gales threaten to break
over the calm drizzle.
the wind picks up,
and her hair cascades and fans around her wild face.
just a light breeze at first:
the calm before the storm.
then her tears fall thicker and faster,
her breathing gets louder and stronger.
she promised a storm
and, here it is.

outside the wind beats hard and low,

the thunder rolls like moving mountains,

a flash of lightning in her sparkling eyes.

her rage pours out like the tempest outdoors.

the tormenting rain drowned out by her screams.

so quickly it comes,

as quickly it goes.

the anger subsides, the thunder is silenced;

replaced by an anguished shower.

and she goes to sleep swimming in tears,

mirrored in drops that stroke her

windowpane.

Meg, 20 years old, From Bury, Greater Manchester. Currently studying Philosophy at University. Avid writer with a passion for poetry.

# John Robinson

## Snow on the Roses

I dream occasionally of that Summer
When I waited in the rain
For the bus that called at your house
Oh, to be sixteen again
Sometimes it feels like the golden days
Were only passing through
There's snow on the roses
But I still love you

It's cold today darling
Though the ice has been and gone
Aches and pains to be expected
Now we're eighty winters on
And yet when I look into your eyes
I can't help but feel new
There's snow on the roses
But I still love you

But we're entering the twilight
The parts hidden by the frame
Time shows no mercy
Tears hold no shame
We're looking through life's telescope

At a disappearing view
There's snow on the roses
But I still love you

I wouldn't change a second of this
It's largely been a blast
One day we'll walk in sunshine
And perfect shadows will be cast
For now I'll stick the kettle on
And make another brew
There's snow on the roses
    But I still love you

---

John is a designer, doodler and would-be poet based in Marple. He took to writing poetry at school when he realised his massive ape like fingers would mean he'd never make it as a guitarist/songwriter. John has had several poems published in the past and writes and publishes his own small collections through social media. He writes mainly about the wonders of nature and growing old.

# Susan Sandilands

## Lunatic

wide-eyes / electric bug
static hair / puffed up mug

gentle fingers / soft tongue
tightly bound / loosely strung

puckered lips / doe-eyed lamb
raging bull / open clam

heart thumping / veins pulsating
head spinning / disc rotating

sitting / staring / rocking / rolling
I am lunatic / I am lu-na-tic

---

Susan Sandilands is a keen experimental poet whose work is fundamentally influenced by the tumultuous effects of her Bipolar Disorder. Sue is soon to complete her M.A. in Creative Writing at the University of Salford in the UK.

# Albert Van Skywalker

## Costa Del Salford

I adore the roar of the ocean, the salted sun kissed breeze
A stroll down the shore, in my shades and shorts: sangria
sipped with ease
But sadly I'm stuck in Salford
And its minus 12 degrees

---

Albert Van Skywalker is a one man mosh pit; a phenomenon, yet somewhat of an enigma- a mophenigma. Albert had an epiphany, which was removed following surgery. During his period of respite he began writing limericks on the walls of restaurants where he discovered his love of the rhyming word. And Chow Mein

# Anthony Smith

## Dragged up proper

We was dragged up proper
One penny sweets from happy shopper
Sonic in 2D, football in the streets
grey clothes like Roy cropper
No I pad's we played hide an seek and British bulldog
We planted whoopee cushions
pulled fingers and blamed it on the bull frogs
In with the cool crew which wasn't very cool
Setting fire to doo doo, to put out with your new shoes
Knock a door run in the afternoon
We rode our bikes until the sun went down
At every other party there was a stupid looking clown
Fifty pence mix up on the weekend, those were the dreams man
On your birthday it was a double ninety nine from the ice
cream man
Catching a ride on the back of the van as it left the avenue
What health and safety?
Those were the days and I miss it greatly
Nineties tunes, jackets of Chicago bulls and L'A Lakers
Jumping off at Red Rock with the risk takers
Garden trotting and playing tag
Curby and when having a joke was a blag
Five of us puffing on a fag

We laughed at ourselves as well as others
Summer holidays bike rides with cousins and brothers
Street lights came on, mothers calls came out
Over the sound of slurping ice pops and crunching crisps
Cheeky risks of always waiting until the third shout from mum
Not be the first one called in, because that's not cool man!
Peanut butter and jam or banana butties
For a luxury we had cookies
Dad's at the bookies
Mum has got the Sunday dinner on
Apple pie and custard with a hint of cinnamon
We had bins without wheels
We listened for the milk mans clink of fresh milk
At six a.m. we waited to eat our frosted flakes
Simple things pleased us
Like mums cooking and ducking and diving
Throwing stones at paddy's window because he popped our ball
In front of us with a screw driver, miserable git!
We hit his car again and again and we'll do it again
Yawning on the way to school
Soon awake when the football landed in the playground
Wembley and ten and your dead kept us entertained
The one thing that made us forget about a cut leg was a nutmeg
We didn't ask for much we had food in our bellies and plenty
of friends
Shoes on our feet, clothes on our back we didn't care for trends
We messed up the word sorry made amends
Although we all sang about wanting that Mercedes Benz
All we really cared for was the simple things
We was dragged up proper...

Anthony has a love of writing in various forms and enjoys sharing his work on the Manchester Open Mic scene.

# Craig Snelgrove

**Forever young in a memory**

I heard your laugh in a fit of nostalgia,
some trick of the mind in a lonely hour.
This Friday night has been spent watching
old BBC sitcoms and an old Italian film.
I treated myself to some cookies and milk after tea.
It appears to me I've hit a lull in happenings.

In bed I dwell on the vast amount of time that has passed
since I last heard you laugh so hard you struggled to breath,
or when we hurriedly shared a cheeky joint
round the back of your local, taking tokes between kisses,
forever young in a memory of days
I didn't see coming to an end.

---

Craig Snelgrove is a writer from Manchester, England. Craig holds an MA in Creative Writing and his work has previously been published locally in Live from Worktown anthologies and most recently in Worktown Words. Craig is also having work published by The Cabinet of Heed in the coming weeks. Craig currently works in Mental Health.

# Emma Stewart

## Brushstrokes

I never knew the wall of silence was you protecting us from what
you went through
I never knew you not wanting to help me with my homework was
your inability to read and write
I didn't know the drink was your way of sounding out the voices
I didn't know your prejudice was a result of you quitting school at
thirteen and having to provide for your brothers and sisters
You never said much, faded into the sofa you slept on for your
last fifteen years
I only realised after, that your odd comical moments were your
way of saying sorry for being serious all the time
We called you the quiet man, it wasn't so quiet up there, was it,
Dad?
I now know it wasn't me, us and them
And I now understand your rage whenever anyone had the nerve
to use the word bastard around you and the way your body would
shudder and catapult you into your mute state
Your automatic drill sergeant bellow that time I accidentally fell
down the stairs
The odd tenner you'd slide into my hand on the quiet for pocket
money when I knew that was the only money you had in the world
That pained look you had in your face at us judging you and you
not being able to articulate the reason why you would be violent

as you didn't know why

Your gripe with the neighbours that consumed you, that made you want to do unspeakable things

Your feelings of loneliness, hopelessness and self-loathing in a home full of life, laughter and growth that you were unable to get involved in and embrace

I wasn't there for you, the last few weeks, even when you were in hospital, I put my lust, my education, me first

I am just so grateful that my intuition kicked in on your last day here, I knew I had to get that bus to see you

We didn't speak for four hours, not a word passed but I listened to you take your last breaths and tell the dog "get down, I haven't got it in me"

You left your last mark in the brushstrokes of paint on the walls in the back garden

Brushstrokes which were wavy, imperfect, rough around the edges but beautiful.

Just like you, Dad.

---

Emma Stewart is a writer and English teacher from Blackley, North Manchester with a proclivity for all things relating to word-play. Influenced from her mother's good taste in Motown and soul music, inspired by the greats such as Marvin Gaye and The Temps, underpinning a soul-searching mission to write about difficult issues, where we are often scared into silence; striving for interconnectedness amongst fellow creatives and "outcasts". Salford University graduate with scriptwriting specialism.

# John Stirton

## Manchester Poem

A year ago, I made the leap to start a new life!
in South Manchester. How about that?
If I don't chat or seem anxious on messenger there's a good
enough reason for that..

For the sky is brighter and in Whitworth Park the sun is stronger.
I literally know no one all I get told is 'work hard son'.
looking forward to catching up soon. For now I might as well be
at the moon.

Manchester enticed me at 15 the first place i went at 16 to see my
brother in his flat.
Now how about that 10 years later I live in Fallowfield and I
didn't know that.
life changes and I'm a Manc! That after taste lasts for ages like
a pint of Guinness in seven stars when it's raining.

# Ali Stone

## Autumn

Our love weaves through my heart like temperate seasons
An unfolding of summer to winter in slow transition
Writing poetry of love as your literary magician
Calm brush of the breeze on our cheeks
Your beauty leaving my lungs with a gentle wheeze
Leaves of red, yellow, orange and brown leave trees
elegantly stripped
You are the key that fits the lock of my souls crypt
Autumn transitions from summer to winter
Our feet crunch crisp leaves fallen from trees
I hear whisperings of my beautiful singer
Abandoning reality I transition into your poetry thinker
Your pleasure falls upon my lips, a sweetness that still lingers
Daylight hours slowly shorten
Mesmerized how our skin against each other feels like
soft brushed cotton
Temperatures plummet and cool
Our memories sculptured and captured on spool
Fiery red and orange skies, you feed my fuel.

Ali Stone is a local Poet whose writing centres on issues such as Mental Health, Childhood trauma & Love. Her main aim is to offer hope and understanding to others.

# Phil Thornton

**For MES**

These streets are still visited by angry ghosts
Those that never made it
Those that never had a chance to make it
Those that couldn't be arsed making it
Making what or for who?
Fuck that for a game of soldiers!
We make our own history and we don't need
YOUR approval
Mutant wordscapes for Prestwich trip tours
Witch finder, cheap provocateur, rancid priest
The Irwell is thick with the flesh of dead dogs
And Manchester's martyrs still seep through the soil
You are now with them in that smokey saloon
Whiskey teeth and wisdom words for those
Who can channel in to your semaphore frequencies
Much missed misanthrope and sulphate scribe
Mark E Smith Lived

---

Phil Thornton is an author, journalist and community worker from Runcorn. He is the author of 'casuals' and has championed the north west's cultural achievements over the past 30 years.

Navaster Twistree

**Christmas town**

It's raining again in Christmas town,
The lights have gone up and the rains coming down.
People push to look with their hands in glove.
Looking for things for the ones they love.
Silver and gold that's what's on my list.
The men in the shop he will insist.
Too wrap it up in paper with a bow.
Now is the time I really do have to go.
It's still raining in Christmas town.
I'm stood outside and feeling down.
The puddle on the path reflect the light.
Now for a taxi I will have to fight.
Shoppers rush push past me.
Just to be the first in to the taxi.
A car goes by and I get a puddle in the face.
It's time to go and leave this place.
We are all wrapped up in this Christmas town.
I'm getting out before I drown.
It's all too much it's got to stop.
The magic we seek is not in the shop.
It's in the face of a child with a smile.
Not in this town with its tacky style.
The magic it's at home with your family and friends.
All this sparkly town it makes us pretend.

When this fake magic leaves this place.
It will leave behind two nasty tastes.
Sickly sour debit and debt.
Two flavours you can never forget.

Jay Watson

**PANDEMIC!**

This invisible scourge, quietly seeps through our lives, tentatively twisting and turning, ready to pounce, devour and incapacitate its next victim.

It emulates, imitates, contemplates like a cunning devious and purposeful snake, leaving a deadly trail of unsuspecting bait.

The clock's ticking.... Another victim, another kin, another Government bulletin.
As we isolate and meditate steadily, amidst the infernal din;
we are consumed by our guilty sin.

Time inevitability passes, as I now begin to breathe the new air, cleared in this new sphere. Each new inhale of fresh life shouts out a cheer! The new dawn is near!

They'll be no more strife I utter with delight!
With incessant glee I hail I am free!
Free to be me! at last I sing as
I eagerly await what the future may bring...

Jay Watson retired from full time employment in 2016, but is now an Online Business Edupreneur, who tutors English Language/Literature at GCSE and 'A' Level. She has a flare for writing poetry and continues in that vein again, as she explores more topical issues with a view to producing her own Poetry Anthology.

# Gemma Whiteley

## Drink

Drink it all up,
Drink up the late late nights,
Drink in my stories of growing tall,
Drinking in closed groups on the school field,
Drink me all up,
And I might just place down my shield,
And drink you all up too,
*Cheers.*

Smoke it all in,
Smoke in the late night clouds,
Smoke in my tales of teenage sin,
Smoking behind the garages at break,
Smoke me all in,
And I'll wrap myself around you like a needy rattlesnake,
And smoke you all in too,
*Inhale.*

Talk it all out,
Talk it out in midnight ramblings,
Talk about the best bits of your youth,
Talking in hushed rushes at the back of class,
Talk me delirious,
And I'll stop with the miss mysterious,

And talk you deaf too,
*After you…*

Touch every inch,
Touch me until the sun never sets again,
Touch through every scar and mark left by growing pains,
Touching a shoulder by chance on the stairs of c block,
Touch me non stop,
And I'll happily touch your hardened …
And touch you tender too,
*sweat.*

Fall far and deep,
Fall freely into the darkest of dark,
Fall down every memory laced lane of that childhood game,
Falling down often and standing back scarred,
Fall for me hard,
And I'll fall for you,
And fall far together we will,
Even if it is to be a short lived thrill,
Drink with me?

---

Gemma Whiteley is a Manchester based actor, director and writer originally from Teesside. She trained in Northampton and began performing her spoken word pieces in Manchester in the last year. She has performed for Speak, Switchblade, Sayin and her work has been published online by The Howling Press.

## Zoe Ann Xenophontos

Good morning to my handsome man
I know you're struggling right now.....
Remember though my love you really can.....
Do anything you set your mind to so take a bow.....

Life is very strange and crazy at the moment.....
Though there is something to still  smile about....
I love you Simon so we WILL  have enjoyment....
You know i shall forever be so very devout ....

So please always try to remember my dear......
I'm here for the rough as well as the smooth....
You really do have nothing to fear.....
Every day ill love you more and try to improve......

Together we can overcome whatever life throws at us....
Strengthened by God's grace and love....
I shall always endeavour to dress to mpress ....
I sincerely believe you've been sent from heaven above.....

All my love always Zoe Ann Xenophontos
Written especially for you
On 12 th August 2020
11 months since we met......

Zoe was born in Manchester in 1974 and is the eldest of ten children, her surname comes from her Greek Cypriot grandad. She is a practising Roman Catholic and is mother to a 26 year old daughter named Danielle.

# About the Editor

James P. Wagner (Ishwa) is an editor, publisher, award-winning fiction writer, essayist, historian performance poet, and alum twice over (BA & MALS) of Dowling College. He is the publisher for Local Gems Poetry Press and the Senior Founder and President of the Bards Initiative. He is also the founder and Grand Laureate of Bards Against Hunger, a series of poetry readings and anthologies dedicated to gathering food for local pantries that operates in over a dozen states. His most recent individual collection of poetry is *Everyday Alchemy*. He was the Long Island, NY National Beat Poet Laureate from 2017-2019. He was the Walt Whitman Bicentennial Convention Chairman and teaches poetry workshops at the Walt Whitman Birthplace State Historic Site. James has edited over 60 poetry anthologies and hosted book launch events up and down the East Coast. He was named the National Beat Poet Laureate of the United States from 2020-2021.

Local Gems Poetry Press is a small Long Island based poetry press    dedicated to spreading poetry through performance and the written word. Local Gems believes that poetry is the voice of the people, and as the sister organization of the Bards Initiative, believes that poetry can be used to make a difference.

Local Gems has published over 250 titles.

www.localgemspoetrypress.com

Made in the USA
Monee, IL
13 January 2021

55414428R00069